THE PYTHON BIBLE

VOLUME FOUR

MACHINE LEARNING

By

FLORIAN DEDOV

Copyright © 2019

TABLE OF CONTENT

INTRODUCTION

With this book, we get into some really advanced territory and things get more and more complicated. In the last book, we were learning about data science and data analysis. We now know how to analyze and visualize big data sets. But except for some statistical values we didn't really extract any knowledge out of the data and we were certainly not able to predict future data.

This is where the topic of this book comes into play – *machine learning*. It's a much hyped term and nowadays it can be found almost everywhere. In robots, video games, the stock market, home appliances or even in cars. And it's constantly growing. The development of artificial intelligences can't be stopped and it bears almost unlimited potential (for both – good and evil). The people who don't educate themselves on this matter will be overrun by the development instead of benefiting from it.

Python is definitely the language that dominates the AI market. Of course, artificial intelligences are developed in all sorts of languages but Python has become the *lingua franca* of machine learning in the past few years. Therefore, if you want to be part of this future, you will need to be fluent in Python and get a good understanding of machine learning.

THIS BOOK

In this volume of The Python Bible series, we will dig deep into the machine learning realm and the Python language. We will train and apply complex machine learning models and at the end you will be able to develop and optimize your own AI suited for your specific tasks.

What you will need for this book is the knowledge from the previous three volumes. You will need to be fluent in the basic and intermediate concepts of the Python language. Also, you will need some basic understanding of data science and the libraries *NumPy, Pandas* and *Matplotlib*. If you have already read volume one to three, you are good to go. A decent understanding of mathematics (high school level) is definitely beneficial.

We will start by discussing what machine learning actually is and what types there are. Then, we will install the necessary modules and start with the programming part. First, we will look at linear regression, which is a pretty basic statistical machine learning model. After that, we will cover classification, clustering and support vector machines. Then, we will discuss neural networks and build a model that predicts handwritten digits. At the end, we will take a look at the optimization of models.

This book is again full of new and more complex information. There is a lot to learn here so stay tuned and code along while reading. This will help you to understand the material better and to practice implementing it. I wish you a lot of fun and success with your journey and this book!

Just one little thing before we start. This book was written for you, so that you can get as much value as possible and learn to code effectively. If you find this book valuable or you think you have learned something new, please write a quick review on Amazon. It is completely free and takes about one minute. But it helps me produce more high quality books, which you can benefit from.

Thank you!

If you are interested in free educational content about programming and machine learning, check out: https://www.neuralnine.com/

1 – WHAT IS MACHINE LEARNING?

As always, before we start to learn how something works, we first want to precisely define what it is, that we are learning about. So what is this hyped concept of *machine learning*? I will not try to give you some sophisticated and complex scientific definition here. We will try to explain it as simply as possible.

What machine learning is fundamentally is just the *science,* in which we focus on teaching machines or computers to perform certain tasks without being given specific instructions. We want our machines to learn how to do something themselves without explaining it to them.

In order to do this, we oftentimes look at how the human brain works and try to design virtual brains that work in a similar manner.

Notice that machine learning and artificial intelligence are not the same. Artificial intelligence is a broad field and every system that can learn and solve problems might be considered an AI. Machine learning is *one specific approach* to this broad field. In machine learning the AI doesn't receive any instructions. It isn't static and it doesn't follow clear and strict steps to solve problems. It's dynamic and restructures itself.

SUPERVISED LEARNING

In machine learning we have different approaches or types. The two main approaches are *supervised learning* and *unsupervised learning*. So let's first talk about supervised learning.

Here, we give our model a set of inputs and also the corresponding outputs, which are the desired results. In this way, the model learns to match certain inputs to certain outputs and it adjusts its structure. It learns to make connections between what was put in and what the desired output is. It understands the correlation. When trained well enough, we can use the model to make predictions for inputs that we don't know the results for.

Classic supervised learning algorithms are regressions, classifications and support vector machines.

UNSUPERVISED LEARNING

With unsupervised learning on the other hand, we don't give our model the desired results while training. Not because we don't want to but because we don't know them. This approach is more like a kind of pattern recognition. We give our model a set of input data and it then has to look for patterns in it. Once the model is trained, we can put in new data and our model will need to make decisions.

Since the model doesn't get any information about classes or results, it has to work with similarities and patterns in the data and categorize or cluster it by itself.

Classic unsupervised learning algorithms are clustering, anomaly detection and some applications of neural networks.

REINFORCEMENT LEARNING

Then there is a third type of machine learning called *reinforcement learning*. Here we create some model with a random structure. Then we just observe what it does and reinforce or encourage it, when we like what it does. Otherwise, we can also give some negative feedback. The more our model does what we want it to do, the more we reinforce it and the more "rewards" it gets. This might happen in form of a number or a grade, which represents the so-called *fitness* of the model.

In this way, our model learns what is right and what is wrong. You can imagine it a little bit like natural selection and survival of the fittest. We can create 100 random models and kill the 50 models that perform worst. Then the remaining 50 reproduce and the same process repeats. These kinds of algorithms are called *genetic algorithms.*

Classic reinforcement learning algorithms are genetic or evolutional algorithms.

Deep Learning

Another term that is always confused with machine learning is *deep learning*. Deep learning however is just one area of machine learning, namely the one, which works with neural networks. Neural networks are a very comprehensive and complex topic. Even though there is a chapter about them in this book, we won't be able to dig too deep into the details here. Maybe I will write a separate volume which just focuses only on neural networks in the future.

Fields of Application

Actually, it would be easier to list all the areas in which machine learning doesn't get applied rather than the fields of application. Despite that, we will take a quick look at some of the major areas, in which machine learning gets applied.

- Research
- Autonomous Cars
- Spacecraft
- Economics and Finance
- Medical and Healthcare
- Physics, Biology, Chemistry
- Engineering
- Mathematics
- Robotics
- Education
- Forensics

- Police and Military
- Marketing
- Search Engines
- GPS and Pathfinding Systems
- ...

We could go on forever. I think it is very clear why we should educate ourselves in this area. With this book, you are going into the right direction.

WHY PYTHON?

Now before we go on to the next chapters, let's once again address the question of why we should use Python for machine learning instead of another language. I already mentioned that it has become the *lingua franca* of machine learning. This means that it has become the main language in this field. You might compare it to English in the western world.

There are also other languages like R, MATLAB or LISP which may be considered competition of Python but they are quite specialized for one specific field of application, whereas Python is a general-purpose language.

Python's community is great and it is massively gaining popularity. The language is simple, easy to learn, easy to use and offers a huge arsenal of powerful open-source libraries for data science, scientific computing and machine learning. Of course other languages have their advantages over Python, but for the field of machine learning there is probably no better choice than Python at the current moment.

2 – Installing Modules

Again, before we get into the coding, we will need to install the modules and libraries that we are going to use. If you have read volume three of this series, you will already be familiar with the first three. Nevertheless, we are going to discuss them quickly one more time.

NumPy

The *NumPy* module allows us to efficiently work with vectors, matrices and multi-dimensional arrays. It is crucial for linear algebra and numerical analysis. It basically replaces the primitive and inefficient Python *list* with very powerful *NumPy arrays*.

Matplotlib

On top of NumPy, we have *Matplotlib*. This library is responsible for plotting graphs and visualizing our data. It offers numerous types of plotting, styles and graphs.

Pandas

Pandas offers us a powerful data structure named *data frame*. You can imagine it to be a bit like a mix of an Excel table and an SQL database table.

This library allows us to efficiently work with our huge amounts of interrelated data. We can merge, reshape, filter and query our data. We can iterate over it and we can read and write into files like CSV, XLSX and more. Also, it is very powerful when we work with databases, due to the similar structure of the tables.

Pandas is highly compatible with NumPy and Matplotlib, since it builds on them. We can easily convert data from one format to the other.

SCIKIT-LEARN

Now, the first new library of this book is *scikit-learn.* This is probably the most important Python library for traditional machine learning. It features classification, regression and clustering algorithms. Also, it allows us to work with support vector machines and more. Scikit-learn is designed to work with NumPy and Matplotlib, which will make everything much easier for us.

TENSORFLOW

Tensorflow is one of the most popular machine learning frameworks out there and it was developed by Google. It is a whole ecosystem for developing modern deep learning models. This means that it is mainly used for the development and training of models that use neural networks. It also has its own data structures and ways of visualizing data.

INSTALLING MODULES WITH PIP

We now need to install our models. In this book, we are using *pip* to do that.

```
pip install numpy
pip install matplotlib
pip install pandas
pip install scikit-learn
pip install tensorflow
```

3 – LINEAR REGRESSION

The easiest and most basic machine learning algorithm is *linear regression*. It will be the first one that we are going to look at and it is a supervised learning algorithm. That means that we need both – inputs and outputs – to train the model.

MATHEMATICAL EXPLANATION

Before we get into the coding, let us talk about the mathematics behind this algorithm.

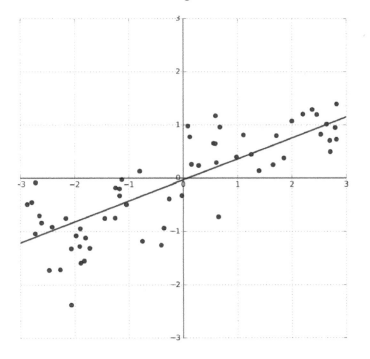

In the figure above, you see a lot of different points, which all have an x-value and a y-value. The x-value is called the *feature*, whereas the y-value is our *label*. The label is the result for our feature. Our *linear regression model* is represented by the blue line that goes straight through our data. It is placed so that it is as close as possible to all points at the same time. So we "trained" the line to fit the existing points or the existing data.

The idea is now to take a new x-value without knowing the corresponding y-value. We then look at the line and find the resulting y-value there, which the model predicts for us. However, since this line is quite generalized, we will get a relatively inaccurate result.

However, one must also mention that linear models only really develop their effectiveness when we are dealing with numerous features (i.e. higher dimensions).

If we are applying this model to data of schools and we try to find a relation between missing hours, learning time and the resulting grade, we will probably get a less accurate result than by including 30 parameters. Logically, however, we then no longer have a straight line or flat surface but a hyperplane. This is the equivalent to a straight line, in higher dimensions.

LOADING DATA

To get started with our code, we first need data that we want to work with. Here we use a dataset from UCI.

Link:
https://archive.ics.uci.edu/ml/datasets/student+performance

This is a dataset which contains a lot of information about student performance. We will use it as sample data for our models.

We download the ZIP-file from the *Data Folder* and extract the file student-mat.csv from there into the folder in which we code our script.

Now we can start with our code. First of all, we will import the necessary libraries.

```
import numpy as np
import pandas as pd
import matplotlib.pyplot as plt
from sklearn.linear_model import
LinearRegression
from sklearn.model_selection import
train_test_split
```

Besides the imports of the first three libraries that we already know, we have two more imports that are new to us. First, we import the *LinearRegression module*. This is the module that we will use for creating, training and using our regression model.

Additionally, we import the *train_test_split* module, which we will use to prepare and split our data.

Our first action is to load the data from the CSV file into a Pandas DataFrame. We do this with the function read_csv.

```
data = pd.read_csv('student-mat.csv',
sep=';')
```

It is important that we change our separator to semicolon, since the default separator for CSV files is a comma and our file is separated by semicolons.

In the next step, we think about which features (i.e. columns) are relevant for us, and what exactly we want to predict. A description of all features can be found on the previously mentioned website. In this example, we will limit ourselves to the following columns:

```
Age, Sex, Studytime, Absences, G1, G2, G3
(label)
```

```
data = data[['age', 'sex', 'studytime',
              'absences', 'G1', 'G2', 'G3']]
```

The columns *G1, G2* and *G3* are the three grades that the students get. Our goal is to predict the third and final grade by looking at the other values like first grade, age, sex and so on.

Summarized that means that we only select these columns from our DataFrame, out of the 33 possible. *G3* is our label and the rest are our features. Each feature is an axis in the coordinate system and each point is a record, that is, one row in the table.

But we have a little problem here. The *sex* feature is not numeric, but stored as *F (for female)* or *M (for male)*. But for us to work with it and register it in the coordinate system, we have to convert it into numbers.

```
data['sex'] = data['sex'].map({'F': 0, 'M': 1})
```

We do this by using the *map* function. Here, we map a dictionary to our feature. Each *F* becomes a zero and every *M* becomes a one. Now we can work with it.

Finally, we define the column of the desired label as a variable to make it easier to work with.

```
prediction = 'G3'
```

PREPARING DATA

Our data is now fully loaded and selected. However, in order to use it as training and testing data for our model, we have to reformat them. The sklearn models do not accept Pandas data frames, but only NumPy arrays. That's why we turn our features into an x-array and our label into a y-array.

```
X = np.array(data.drop([prediction], 1))
Y = np.array(data[prediction])
```

The method *np.array* converts the selected columns into an array. The *drop* function returns the data frame without the specified column. Our *X* array now contains all of our columns, except for the final grade. The final grade is in the *Y* array.

In order to train and test our model, we have to split our available data. The first part is used to get the hyperplane to fit our data as well as possible. The second part then checks the accuracy of the prediction, with previously unknown data.

```
X_train, X_test, Y_train, Y_test =
train_test_split(X, Y, test_size=0.1)
```

With the function *train_test_split*, we divide our *X* and *Y* arrays into four arrays. The order must be exactly as shown here. The *test_size* parameter specifies what percentage of records to use for testing. In this case, it is 10%. This is also a good and recommended value. We do this to test how accurate it is with data that our model has never seen before.

TRAINING AND TESTING

Now we can start training and testing our model. For that, we first define our model.

```
model = LinearRegression()
model.fit(X_train, Y_train)
```

By using the constructor of the *LinearRegression* class, we create our model. We then use the *fit* function and pass our training data. Now our model is already trained. It has now adjusted its hyperplane so that it fits all of our values.

In order to test how well our model performs, we can use the *score* method and pass our testing data.

```
accuracy = model.score(X_test, Y_test)
print(accuracy)
```

Since the splitting of training and test data is always random, we will have slightly different results on each run. An average result could look like this:

```
0.9130676521162756
```

Actually, 91 percent is a pretty high and good accuracy. Now that we know that our model is somewhat reliable, we can enter new data and predict the final grade.

```
X_new = np.array([[18, 1, 3, 40, 15, 16]])
Y_new = model.predict(X_new)
print(Y_new)
```

Here we define a new NumPy array with values for our features in the right order. Then we use the *predict* method, to calculate the likely final grade for our inputs.

```
[17.12142363]
```

In this case, the final grade would probably be 17.

VISUALIZING CORRELATIONS

Since we are dealing with high dimensions here, we can't draw a graph of our model. This is only possible in two or three dimensions. However, what we can visualize are relationships between individual features.

```
plt.scatter(data['studytime'], data['G3'])
plt.title("Correlation")
plt.xlabel("Study Time")
plt.ylabel("Final Grade")
plt.show()
```

Here we draw a scatter plot with the function scatter, which shows the relationship between the learning time and the final grade.

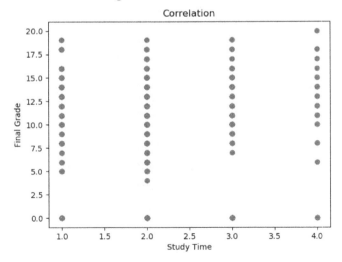

In this case, we see that the relationship is not really strong. The data is very diverse and you cannot see a clear pattern.

```
plt.scatter(data['G2'], data['G3'])
plt.title("Correlation")
plt.xlabel("Second Grade")
plt.ylabel("Final Grade")
plt.show()
```

However, if we look at the correlation between the second grade and the final grade, we see a much stronger correlation.

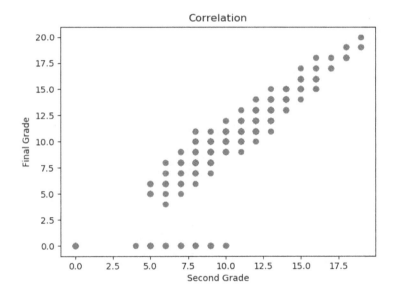

Here we can clearly see that the students with good second grades are very likely to end up with a good final grade as well. You can play around with the different columns of this data set if you want to.

4 – CLASSIFICATION

With regression we now predicted specific output-values for certain given input-values. Sometimes, however, we are not trying to predict outputs but to categorize or classify our elements. For this, we use *classification* algorithms.

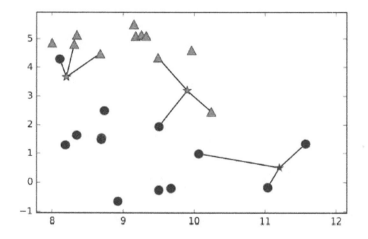

In the figure above, we see one specific kind of classification algorithm, namely the *K-Nearest-Neighbor* classifier. Here we already have a decent amount of classified elements. We then add a new one (represented by the stars) and try to predict its class by looking at its nearest neighbors.

CLASSIFICATION ALGORITHMS

There are various different classification algorithms and they are often used for predicting medical data or other real life use-cases. For example, by providing a large amount of tumor samples, we can classify if a tumor is benign or malignant with a pretty high certainty.

K-NEAREST-NEIGHBORS

As already mentioned, by using the K-Nearest-Neighbors classifier, we assign the class of the new object, based on its nearest neighbors. The *K* specifies the amount of neighbors to look at. For example, we could say that we only want to look at the one neighbor who is nearest but we could also say that we want to factor in 100 neighbors.

Notice that *K* shouldn't be a multiple of the number of classes since it might cause conflicts when we have an equal amount of elements from one class as from the other.

NAIVE-BAYES

The *Naive Bayes* algorithm might be a bit confusing when you encounter it the first time. However, we are only going to discuss the basics and focus more on the implementation in Python later on.

Outlook	Temperture	Humidity	Windy	Play
Sunny	Hot	High	False	No

Sunny	Hot	High	True	No
Rainy	Mild	High	False	No
Rainy	Hot	High	True	No
Overcast	Hot	Normal	True	Yes
Sunny	Hot	Normal	True	Yes
Sunny	Mild	High	True	Yes
Overcast	Cold	Normal	True	No
...	...	...	...	...

Imagine that we have a table like the one above. We have four input values (which we would have to make numerical of course) and one label or output. The two classes are *Yes* and *No* and they indicate if we are going to play outside or not.

What *Naive Bayes* now does is to write down all the probabilities for the individual scenarios. So we would start by writing the general probability of playing and not playing. In this case, we only play three out of eight times and thus our probability of playing will be 3/8 and the probability of not playing will be 5/8.

Also, out of the five times we had a high humidity we only played once, whereas out of the three times it was normal, we played twice. So our probability for playing when we have a high humidity is 1/5 and for playing when we have a medium humidity is 2/3. We go on like that and note all the probabilities we have in our table. To then get the classification for a new entry, we multiply the probabilities together and end up with a prediction.

Logistic Regression

Another popular classification algorithm is called *logistic regression*. Even though the name says *regression*, this is actually a classification algorithm. It looks at probabilities and determines how likely it is that a certain event happens (or a certain class is the right one), given the input data. This is done by plotting something similar to a logistic growth curve and splitting the data into two.

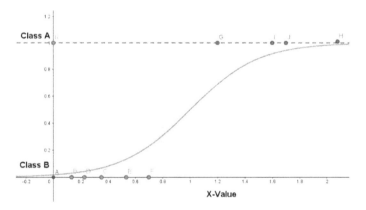

Since we are not using a line (and thus our model is not linear), we are also preventing mistakes caused by outliers.

Decision Trees

With *decision tree* classifiers, we construct a decision tree out of our training data and use it to predict the classes of new elements.

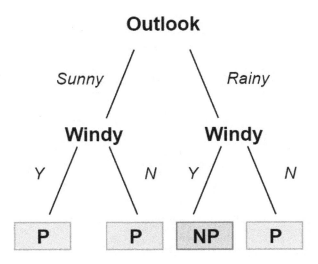

This classification algorithm requires very little data preparation and it is also very easy to understand and visualize. On the other hand, it is very easy to be *overfitting* the model. Here, the model is very closely matched to the training data and thus has worse chances to make a correct prediction on new data.

RANDOM FOREST

The last classification algorithm of this chapter is the *random forest* classifier. It is based on decision trees. What it does is creating a *forest* of multiple decision trees. To classify a new object, all the various trees determine a class and the most frequent result gets chosen. This makes the result more accurate and it also prevents overfitting. It is also more suited to handle data sets with higher dimensions. On the other hand, since the generation of the forest is *random*, you have very little control over your model.

LOADING DATA

Now let us get into the code. In this example, we will get our data directly from the sklearn module. For the program we need the following imports:

```
import numpy as np
from sklearn.model_selection import
train_test_split
from sklearn.neighbors import
KNeighborsClassifier
from sklearn.datasets import load_breast_cancer
```

At the last import, we import a dataset containing data on breast cancer. Also notice that we are only importing the *KNeighborsClassifier* for now.

```
data = load_breast_cancer()

print(data.feature_names)
print(data.target_names)
```

We load the data with the *load_breast_cancer* function and get the names of the features and targets. Our features are all parameters that should help to determine the label or the target. For the targets, we have two options in this dataset: *malignant* and *benign*.

PREPARING DATA

Again, we convert our data back into NumPy arrays and split them into training and test data.

```
X = np.array(data.data)
Y = np.array(data.target)
```

```
X_train, X_test, Y_train, Y_test =
train_test_split(X,Y,test_size=0.1)
```

The data attribute refers to our features and the target attribute points to the classes or labels. We again choose a test size of ten percent.

TRAINING AND TESTING

We start by first defining our K-Nearest-Neighbors classifier and then training it.

```
knn = KNeighborsClassifier(n_neighbors=5)
knn.fit(X_train, Y_train)
```

The *n_neighbors* parameter specifies how many neighbor points we want to consider. In this case, we take five. Then we test our model again for its accuracy.

```
accuracy = knn.score(X_test, Y_test)
print(accuracy)
```

We get a pretty decent accuracy for such a complex task.

```
0.9649122807017544
```

THE BEST ALGORITHM

Now let's put all the classification algorithms that we've discussed up until now to use and see which one performs best.

```
from sklearn.neighbors import
KNeighborsClassifier
from sklearn.naive_bayes import GaussianNB
from sklearn.linear_model import
LogisticRegression
from sklearn.tree import DecisionTreeClassifier
from sklearn.ensemble import
RandomForestClassifier
```

Of course, we need to import all the modules first. We can then create five different classifiers to train and test them with the exact same data.

```
clf1 = KNeighborsClassifier(n_neighbors=5)
clf2 = GaussianNB()
clf3 = LogisticRegression()
clf4 = DecisionTreeClassifier()
clf5 = RandomForestClassifier()

clf1.fit(X_train, Y_train)
clf2.fit(X_train, Y_train)
clf3.fit(X_train, Y_train)
clf4.fit(X_train, Y_train)
clf5.fit(X_train, Y_train)

print(clf1.score(X_test, Y_test))
print(clf2.score(X_test, Y_test))
print(clf3.score(X_test, Y_test))
print(clf4.score(X_test, Y_test))
print(clf5.score(X_test, Y_test))
```

When you run this program a couple of times, you will notice that we can't really say which algorithm is the best. Every time we run this script, we will see different results, at least for this specific data set.

PREDICTING LABELS

Again, we can again make predictions for new, unknown data. The chance of success in the classification is even very high. We just need to pass an array of input values and use the *predict function*.

```
X_new = np.array([[...]])
Y_new = clf.predict(X_new)
```

Unfortunately, visualizing the data is not possible here because we have 30 features and cannot draw a 30-dimensional coordinate system.

5 – SUPPORT VECTOR MACHINES

Now things get mathematically a bit more demanding. This chapter is about *Support Vector Machines*. These are very powerful, very efficient machine learning algorithms and they even achieve much better results than neural networks in some areas. We are again dealing with classification here but the methodology is quite different.

What we are looking for is a *hyperplane* that distinctly classifies our data points and has the maximum margin to all of our points. We want our model to be as generalized as possible.

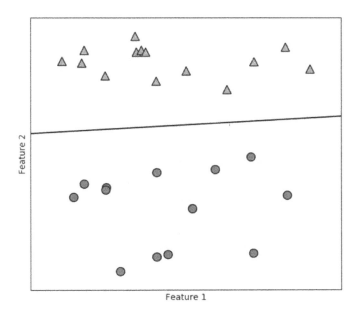

In the graph above the model is very general and the line is the optimal function to separate our data. We can use an endless amount of lines to separate the two classes but we don't want to overfit our model so that it only works for the data we already have. We also want it to work for unknown data.

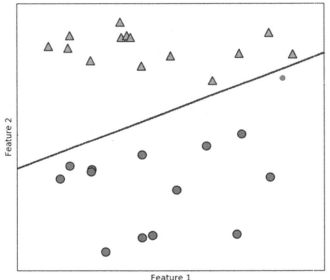

Feature 1

Here our model also separates the data we already have perfectly. But we've got a new red data point here. When we just look at this with our intuition it is obvious that this point belongs to the orange triangles. However, our model classifies it as a blue circle because it is overfitting our current data.

To find our perfect line we are using so-called *support vectors*, which are parallel lines.

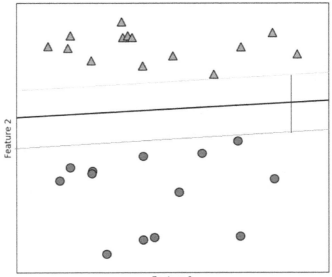

Feature 1

We are looking for the two points that are the farthest away from the other class. In between of those, we draw our hyperplane so that the distance to both points is the same and as large as possible. The two parallel lines are the support vectors. In between the orange and the blue line there are no data points. This is our margin. We want this margin to be as big as possible because it makes our predictions more reliable.

KERNELS

The data we have looked at so far is relatively easy to classify because it is clearly separated. Such data can almost never be found in the real world. Also, we are oftentimes working in higher dimensions with many features. This makes things more complicated.

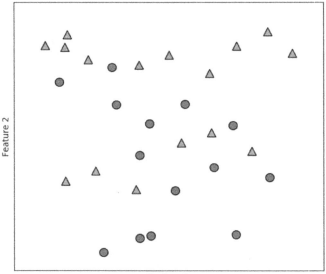

Feature 1

Data taken from the real world often looks like this in figure. Here it is impossible to draw a straight line, and even a quadratic or cubic function does not help us here. In such cases we can use so-called *kernels*. These add a new dimension to our data. By doing that, we hope to increase the complexity of the data and possibly use a hyperplane as a separator.

Notice that the kernel (a.k.a. the additional dimension) should be derived from the data that we already have. We are just making it more abstract. A kernel is not some random feature but a combination of the features we already have.

We can define our kernel to be whatever we want. For example, we could define it as the result of dividing feature one by feature two. But that wouldn't be reasonable or helpful. Therefore, there are pre-defined and effective kernels that we can choose from.

SOFT MARGIN

Sometimes, we will encounter statistical outliers in our data. It would be very easy to draw a hyperplane that separates the data into the classes, if it wasn't for these outliers.

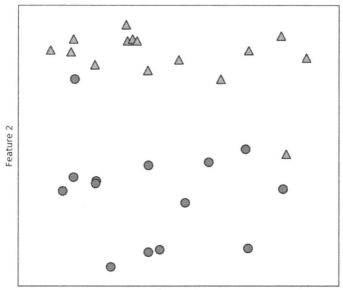

Feature 1

In the figure above, you can see such a data set. We can see that almost all of the orange triangles are in the top first third, whereas almost all the blue dots are in the bottom two thirds. The problem here is with the outliers.

Now instead of using a kernel or a polynomial function to solve this problem, we can define a so-called *soft margin*. With this, we allow for conscious misclassification of outliers in order to create a more accurate model. Caring too much about these outliers would again mean overfitting the model.

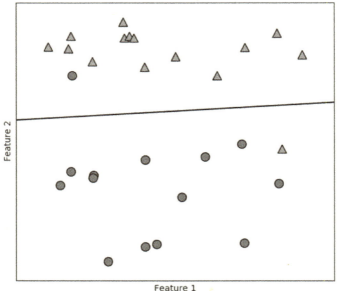

Feature 1

As you can see, even though we are misclassifying two data points our model is very accurate.

LOADING DATA

Now that we understand how SVMs work, let's get into the coding. For this machine learning algorithm, we are going to once again use the breast cancer data set. We will need the following imports:

```
from sklearn.svm import SVC
from sklearn.datasets import load_breast_cancer
from sklearn.neighbors import
KNeighborsClassifier
from sklearn.model_selection import
train_test_split
```

Besides the libraries we already know, we are importing the *SVC* module. This is the support vector classifier that we are going to use as our model. Notice that we are also importing the *KNeighborsClassifier* again, since we are going to compare the accuracies at the end.

```
data = load_breast_cancer()

X = data.data
Y = data.target

X_train, X_test, Y_train, Y_test =
train_test_split(X, Y, test_size=0.1,
random_state=30)
```

This time we use a new parameter named *random_state*. It is a seed that always produces the exact same split of our data. Usually, the data gets split randomly every time we run the script. You can use whatever number you want here. Each number creates a certain split which doesn't change no matter how many times we run the script. We do this in order to be able to objectively compare the different classifiers.

TRAINING AND TESTING

So first we define our support vector classifier and start training it.

```
model = SVC(kernel='linear', C=3)
model.fit(X_train, Y_train)
```

We are using two parameters when creating an instance of the SVC class. The first one is our *kernel* and the second one is *C* which is our soft margin. Here we choose a *linear* kernel and allow for three misclassifications. Alternatively we could choose *poly, rbf, sigmoid, precomputed* or a self-defined kernel. Some are more effective in certain situations but also a lot more time-intensive than linear kernels.

```
accuracy = model.score(X_test, Y_test)
print(accuracy)
```

When we now *score* our model, we will see a very good result.

```
0.9649122807017544
```

Now let's take a look at the *KNeighborsClassifier* with the same *random_state*.

```
knn = KNeighborsClassifier(n_neighbors=5)
knn.fit(X_train, Y_train)

knn_accuracy = knn.score(X_test, Y_test)
print(knn_accuracy)
```

The result is only a tiny bit worse but when the data becomes larger and more complex, we might see a quite bigger difference.

```
0.9473684210526315
```

Play around with different *random_state* parameters. You will see that most of the time the SVC will perform better.

6 – CLUSTERING

Up until now, we have only looked at supervised learning algorithms. *Clustering* however is an unsupervised learning algorithm, which means that we don't have the results for our inputs. We can't tell our model what is right and wrong. It has to find patterns on its own.

The algorithm gets raw data and tries to divide it up into *clusters*. K-Means-Clustering is the method that we are going to use here. Similar to K-Nearest-Neighbors, the *K* states the amount of clusters we want.

HOW CLUSTERING WORKS

The clustering itself works with so-called *centroids*. These are the points, which lie in the center of the respective clusters.

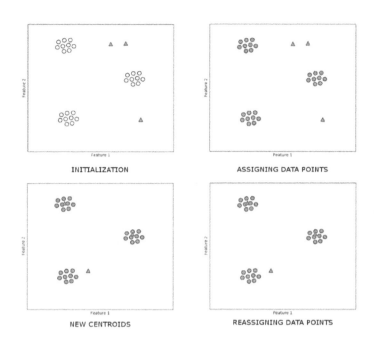

INITIALIZATION

ASSIGNING DATA POINTS

NEW CENTROIDS

REASSIGNING DATA POINTS

The figure above illustrates quite well how clustering works. First, we randomly place the centroids somewhere in our data. This is the *initialization*. Here, we have defined three clusters, which is why we also have three centroids.

Then, we look at each individual data point and assign the cluster of the nearest centroid to it. When we have done this, we continue by realigning our centroids. We place them in the middle of all points of their cluster.

After that, we again reassign the points to the new centroids. We continue doing this over and over again until almost nothing changes anymore. Then we will hopefully end up with the optimal clusters. The result then looks like this:

Feature 1

Of course, you will probably never find data that looks like this in the real world. We are working with much more complex data and much more features (i.e. dimensions).

LOADING DATA

For the clustering algorithm, we will use a dataset of handwritten digits. Since we are using unsupervised learning, we are not going to classify the digits. We are just going to put them into clusters. The following imports are necessary:

```
from sklearn.cluster import KMeans
from sklearn.preprocessing import scale
from sklearn.datasets import load_digits
```

Besides the *KMeans* module and the *load_digits* dataset, we are also importing the function *scale* from the *preprocessing* library. We will use this function for preparing our data.

```
digits = load_digits()
data = scale(digits.data)
```

After loading our dataset we use the *scale* function, to standardize our data. We are dealing with quite large values here and by scaling them down to smaller values we save computation time.

TRAINING AND PREDICTING

We can now train our model in the same way we trained the supervised learning models up until now.

```
clf = KMeans(n_clusters=10, init="random",
n_init=10)
clf.fit(data)
```

Here we are passing three parameters. The first one (*n_clusters*) defines the amount of clusters we want to have. Since we are dealing with the digits 0 to 9, we create ten different clusters.

With the *init* parameter we choose the way of initialization. Here we chose *random*, which obviously means that we just randomly place the centroids somewhere. Alternatively, we could use *k-means++* for intelligent placing.

The last parameter (*n_init*) states how many times the algorithm will be run with different centroid seeds to find the best clusters.

Since we are dealing with unsupervised learning here, scoring the model is not really possible. You won't be able to really score if the model is clustering right or not. We could only benchmark certain statistics like *completeness* or *homogeneity*.

What we can do however is to predict which cluster a new input belongs to.

```
clf.predict([...])
```

In this case, inputting data might be quite hard, since we would need to manually put in all the pixels. You could either try to write a script what converts images into NumPy arrays or you could work with a much simpler data set.

Also, since we are working with huge dimensions here, visualization is quite hard. When you work with two- or three-dimensional data, you can use the Matplotlib knowledge from volume three, in order to visualize your model.

7 – NEURAL NETWORKS

As already mentioned in the beginning, *neural networks* are a very complex and comprehensive topic. Way too comprehensive to cover it in one chapter. For this reason, I will probably write a separate book about neural networks in the future. However, in this chapter, we are going to cover the basics of neural networks and we will build a fully functioning model that classifies handwritten digits properly.

STRUCTURE OF A NEURAL NETWORK

With neural networks we are trying to build our models based on the structure of the human brain, namely with neurons. The human brain is composed of multiple billions of neurons which are interconnected. Neural networks are structures which try to use a similar principle.

INPUT   HIDDEN   OUTPUT

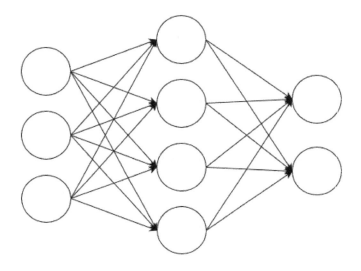

In the figure above, we can see three layers. First the *input layer*, at the end the *output layer* and in between the *hidden layer*.

Obviously the input layer is where our inputs go. There we put all the things which are being entered or sensed by the script or the machine. Basically these are our features.

We can use neural networks to classify data or to act on inputs and the output layer is where we get our results. These results might be a class or action steps. Maybe when we input a high temperature into our model, the output will be the action of cooling down the machine.

All the layers between input and output are called *hidden layers*. They make the model more abstract and more complex. They extend the internal logic. The more hidden layers and neurons you add, the more sophisticated the model gets.

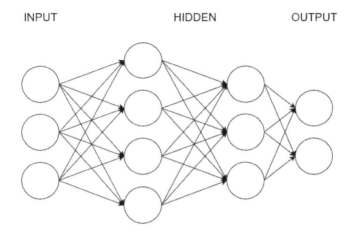

Here for example we have two hidden layers, one with four neurons and one with three neurons. Notice that every neuron of a layer is connected to every neuron of the next layer.

STRUCTURE OF A NEURON

In order to understand how a neural network works in general, we need to understand how the individual neurons work.

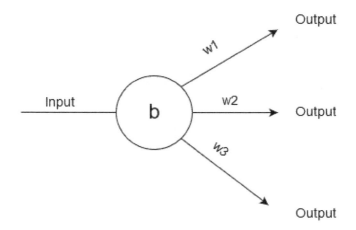

As you can see, every neuron has a certain input, which is either the output of another neuron or the input of the first layer.

This number (which is the input) now gets multiplied by each of the *weights (w1, w2, w3…)*. After that, we subtract the *bias b*. The results of these calculations are the outputs of the neuron.

What I have just explained and what you can see on the picture is an outdated version of a neuron called a *perceptron*. Nowadays, we are using more complex neurons like the *sigmoid neurons* which use more sophisticated activation functions to calculate the outputs.

Now you can maybe imagine to some degree how complex these systems get when we combine hundreds of thousands of these neurons in one network.

How Neural Networks Work

But what has all this to do with artificial intelligence or machine learning? Since neural networks are structures with a huge amount of parameters that can be changed, we can use certain algorithms so that the model can adjust itself. We input our data and the desired outcome. Then the model tries to adjust its weights and biases so that we can get from our inputs to the respective outputs. Since we are dealing with multiple thousands of neurons, we can't do all this manually.

We use different algorithms like *backpropagation* and *gradient descent*, to optimize and train our model. We are not going to deep into the mathematics here. Our focus will be on the coding and the implementation.

Recognizing Handwritten Digits

Up until now, we always used the *sklearn* module for traditional machine learning. Because of that all our examples were quite similar. In this chapter, we will use *Tensorflow*. We will need the following imports:

```
import numpy as np
import tensorflow as tf
import matplotlib.pyplot as plt
```

Loading Data

The handwritten digits data that we are going to use in this chapter is provided by the *Tensorflow Keras* datasets. It is the so-called *MNIST* dataset which contains 70,000 images of handwritten digits in the resolution of 28x28 pixels.

```
mnist = tf.keras.datasets.mnist
(X_train, Y_train), (X_test, Y_test) =
mnist.load_data()
```

The *mnist* class that we import here has the function *load_data*. This function returns two tuples with two elements each. The first tuple contains our training data and the second one our test data. In the training data we can find 60,000 images and in the test data 10,000.

The images are stored in the form of NumPy arrays which contain the information about the individual pixels. Now we need to normalize our data to make it easier to handle.

```
X_train = tf.keras.utils.normalize(X_train)
X_test = tf.keras.utils.normalize(X_test)
```

By normalizing our data with the *normalize* function of the *keras.utils* module, we scale our data down. We standardize it as we have already done in the last chapter. Notice that we are only normalizing the X-values since it wouldn't make a lot of sense to scale down our results, which are the digits from 0 to 9.

BUILDING THE NEURAL NETWORK

We have prepared our data so that we can now start building our network. Tensorflow offers us a very easy way to construct neural networks. We just create a model and then define the individual layers in it.

```
model = tf.keras.models.Sequential()
model.add(tf.keras.layers.Flatten(input_shape=(28,2
8)))
model.add(tf.keras.layers.Dense(units=128,
                         activation='relu'))
model.add(tf.keras.layers.Dense(units=128,
                         activation='relu'))
model.add(tf.keras.layers.Dense(units=10,

        activation=tf.nn.softmax))
```

First we define our model to be a *Sequential*. This is a linear type of model where which is defined layer by layer. Once we have defined the model, we can use the *add* function to add as many different layers as we want.

The first layer that we are adding here is the input layer. In our case, this is a *Flatten* layer. This type of layer flattens the input. As you can see, we have specified the input shape of 28x28 (because of the pixels). What *Flatten* does is to transform this shape into one dimension which would here be 784x1.

All the other layers are of the class *Dense*. This type of layer is the basic one which is connected to every neuron of the neighboring layers. We always specify two parameters here. First, the *units* parameter which states the amount of neurons in this layer and second the *activation* which specifies which activation function we are using.

We have two hidden layers with 128 neurons each. The activation function that we are using here is called *relu* and stands for *rectified linear unit*. This is a very fast and a very simple function. It basically just returns zero whenever our input is negative and the input itself whenever it is positive.

$$f(x) = max(0,x)$$

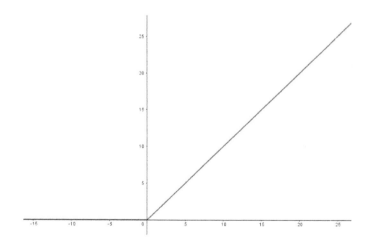

We use it because it is quite simple, quite powerful, very fast and prevents negative values.

For our output layer we only use ten neurons (because we have ten possible digits to classify) and a different activation function. This one is called *softmax* and what it does is it picks output values so that all of our end results add up to one. Because of this we are getting ten different probabilities for each digit, indicating its likelihood.

Our model is now defined but before we can start working with it, we have to compile it first. By doing this we define certain parameters and configure it for training and testing.

```
model.compile(optimizer='adam',
        loss='sparse_categorical_crossentro
py',
        metrics=['accuracy'])
```

Here we define three things, namely the *optimizer*, the *loss function* and the *metrics* that we are interested in. We are not going to go into the math of the *adam* optimizer or the *sparse_categorical_crossentropy* loss function. However, these are very popular choices, especially for tasks like this one.

TRAINING AND TESTING

The training and testing of the model is quite simple and very similar to the way we did it with *sklearn* models.

```
model.fit(X_train, Y_train, epochs=3)
loss, accuracy = model.evaluate(X_test,
Y_test)
print('Loss: ', loss)
print('Accuracy: ', accuracy)
```

We use the *fit* function to train our model but this time we have an additional parameter named *epochs*. The number of epochs is the number of times that we feed the same data into the model over and over again. By using the *evaluate* function, we get two values – *loss* and *accuracy*.

The accuracy is the percentage of correctly classified digits and therefore we want to keep it as high as possible. The loss on the other hand is not a percentage but a summation of the errors made that we want to minimize.

When we run our test, we have a pretty high accuracy around 97 percent.

PREDICTING YOUR OWN DIGITS

Now that we have trained such an awesome model, we of course want to play with it. So what we are going to do is to read in our own images of handwritten digits and predict them with our model.

For this, you can either use software like Paint or Gimp and draw 28x28 pixel images or you can scan digits from real documents into your computer and scale them down to this size. But we will need an additional library here that we haven't installed yet.

```
pip install opencv-python
```

This library is called *OpenCV* and is mainly used for computer vision. However, we will use it in order to read in our images. The import looks a little bit different than the installation.

```
import cv2 as cv
```

Now the only thing we need to prepare is a 28x28 image of a handwritten digit. Then we can start coding.

```
image = cv.imread('digit.png')[:,:,0]
image = np.invert(np.array([image]))
```

We use the *imread* method to read our image into the script. Because of the format we remove the last dimension so that everything matches with the input necessary for the neural network. Also, we need to convert our image into a NumPy array and invert it, since it will confuse our model otherwise.

Finally, we just have to use the *predict* function of our model on our image and see if it works.

```
prediction = model.predict(image)
print("Prediction:
{}".format(np.argmax(prediction)))
plt.imshow(image[0])
plt.show()
```

The prediction we get is an array of the ten different probabilities calculated by the *softmax* activation function. By using the *argmax* method, we get the index of the highest probability, which at the same time is the respective digit.

Last but not least, we use Matplotlibs *imshow* function, to display the image that we just scanned. The result is very satisfying.

Prediction: 7

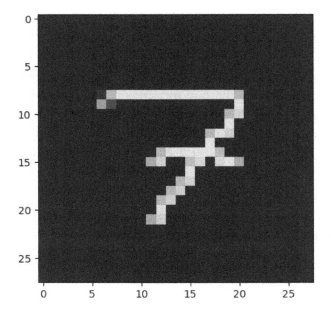

If you are looking for a little challenge, you can try to do the same thing by using a Support Vector Machine. Usually it performs better than a neural network at this particular task. Otherwise just play around with some digits and have fun.

8 – Optimizing Models

In this final chapter we will talk about saving, loading and optimizing our models. Up until now we always loaded our data, trained and tested our model and then used it. But sometimes (as you have probably noticed with neural networks) the training is very time-intensive and we don't want to train the model every time we run the script again. Training it one time is enough.

Serialization

For this reason, there is the concept of *serialization*. We use it to save objects into files during runtime. By doing this, we are not only saving the attributes but the whole state of the object. Because of that, we can load the same object back into a program later and continue working with it.

To work with serialization in Python, we need to import the module *pickle*:

```
import pickle
```

Saving Models

As our example, we will use the breast cancer classification script that uses SVMs.

```python
import pickle
from sklearn.svm import SVC
from sklearn.datasets import
load_breast_cancer
from sklearn.model_selection import
train_test_split

data = load_breast_cancer()

X = data.data
Y = data.target

X_train, X_test, Y_train, Y_test =
train_test_split(X, Y, test_size=0.1)

model = SVC(kernel='linear', C=3)
model.fit(X_train, Y_train)
```

Here we have fully trained our model and we could also go ahead and score it but we don't want to use it right now. We want to save it so that we can use it in the future whenever we need it.

```python
with open('model.pickle', 'wb') as file:
    pickle.dump(model, file)
```

We are opening a file stream in the *write bytes* mode. Then we use the *dump* function of pickle, to save our model into the specified file.

LOADING MODELS

Loading our model is now quite simple. We can write a completely new script and use the model there.

```python
import pickle
```

```python
with open('model.pickle', 'rb') as file:
    model = pickle.load(file)

model.predict([...])
```

Here we open a file stream in the *read bytes* mode and use the *load* function of the pickle module to get the model into our program. We can then just continue and work with it.

OPTIMIZING MODELS

We can use this serialization principle in order to train our model in the best way possible and to optimize it.

```python
best_accuracy = 0

for x in range(2500):
    X_train, X_test, Y_train, Y_test =
train_test_split(X, Y, test_size=0.1)

    model = SVC(kernel='linear', C=3)
    model.fit(X_train, Y_train)
    accuracy = model.score(X_test, Y_test)
    if accuracy > best_accuracy:
        best_accuracy = accuracy
        print("Best accuracy: ", accuracy)
        with open('model.pickle', 'wb') as file:
            pickle.dump(model, file)
```

The concept is quite simple. We define a variable *best_accuracy* which starts with the value zero. Then we run a loop with 2500 iterations and we train our model over and over again with a different split for our data and different seeds.

When we test the model, we check if the accuracy is higher than the highest measured accuracy (starting with zero). If that is the case, we save the model and update the best accuracy. By doing this, we find the model with the highest accuracy.

Notice that we are still only using our training data and our test data. This means that if we take things too far, we might overfit the model, especially with simple datasets. It is not impossible to reach an accuracy of 100% but the question remains if this accuracy also applies to unknown data.

WHAT'S NEXT?

You've come quite far! You've finally finished volume four of this Python Bible series. We covered a lot of machine learning material, from basic linear regression, over support vector machines to neural networks. You have every right to be proud of yourself that you have made it that far.

The skills you possess right now are crucial in today's economy. They are rare and very valuable. You are not only capable of developing advanced Python scripts but also of developing awesome and powerful machine learning models that can be applied to complex real-life problems.

I encourage you to continue your journey. Even though you have already learned quite a lot, we don't stop here. There are a lot of topics to be covered yet and you should not miss out on them. Practice what you've learned, play around and experiment! I wish you a lot of success on your programming journey! Stay tuned and read the next volume, which is about finance!

Last but not least, a little reminder. This book was written for you, so that you can get as much value as possible and learn to code effectively. If you find this book valuable or you think you learned something new, please write a quick review on Amazon. It is completely free and takes about one minute. But it helps me produce more high quality books, which you can benefit from.

Thank you!

NeuralNine

If you are interested in free educational content about programming and machine learning, check out https://www.neuralnine.com/

There we have free blog posts, videos and more for you! Also, you can follow the ***@neuralnine*** Instagram account for daily infographics about programming and AI!

Website: https://www.neuralnine.com/

Instagram: @neuralnine

YouTube: NeuralNine